english
adelante

11 Uses of the Verb "To Be"

English Adelante Copyright © 2019 by P. Jarrett Meek

All rights reserved. No part of this work may be reproduced, recorded, dramatized, or otherwise copied without prior written permission from the author. Clipart from publicdomainvectors.org and openclipart.org.

Printed in the United States of America.

ISBN: 9781793090102

author's note

Inspiration
In 2002, my wife and I moved with our two young daughters to Costa Rica to learn Spanish in preparation for mission work in South America. We were immersed in Costa Rican culture, new people, and a new language. For the first time in our lives, we were outsiders, fish out of water, foreigners in country that was not our own. What could have been a hard experience became one of the most satisfying seasons of our lives as we were befriended by a Costa Rican family who helped us discover their beautiful country, navigate everyday life, and practice Spanish. By far the greatest personal lesson from our time in Costa Rica was being on the receiving end of the hospitality that God intends for us to show to people from other places.

Putting it into Practice
After learning Spanish and living in Latin America for about two years, we returned home to Kansas City with a passion to demonstrate the same Christ-like compassion and hospitality to immigrants in our own city. We moved into an immigrant community and started an English class in our home. That class was the beginning of a new ministry called Mission Adelante that has loved and served immigrants and refugees from many countries since 2005.

A Relational Model
This curriculum, *English Adelante*, is the fruit of our own experiences learning and teaching foreign language, primarily with Spanish-speakers. Our teaching model utilizes native English-speakers as volunteer conversation partners, and this curriculum was designed specifically for use in a classroom with a volunteer:student ratio that approaches 1:1. The benefits of this highly individualized approach include a strong emphasis on relationships, a high value on verbal practice and repetition, and the possibility of customizing the learning experience to the ability level of each student, even withing one classroom. Countless volunteers have served, taught, befriended, and shared the love of Christ with immigrants through our ESL program. After the table of contents, you will find the standard class session outline (2 hours) that we use to teach this curriculum over a 12-week trimester.

11 Uses of the Verb "*To Be*"
The significance of the English verb *To Be* is hard to overstate. It is such a power verb that its meaning and uses connect with five of the most common Spanish verbs including Ser (soy pastor), Estar (estoy feliz), Hacer (hace frío), Tener (tengo hambre), Haber (hay comida). If a person can master the verb *To Be*, they are well on their way to speaking English. As you will see, the 11 uses of *To Be* taught in *English Adelante* represent some of the most common, basic English found in everyday conversations.

QR Codes to Audio
The QR codes you will find on the first page of each lesson will direct students to a page on Mission Adelante's website that has an audio companion to *English Adelante* that students can use with the curriculum to practice outside of class.

I'm excited to offer this resource and pray it will be a useful tool for individuals and organizations who want to serve and share life with people from all places.

Sincerely,
Jarrett Meek

nota del autor

Inspiración
En el año 2002, mi esposa y yo, con nuestras dos hijas, nos mudamos a Costa Rica a estudiar Español, en preparación para un trabajo misionero en Sudamérica. Nos sumergimos en la cultura costarricense, con gente nueva y un idioma nuevo. Por primera vez en la vida nos sentíamos como peces fuera del agua, extranjeros en un país ajeno. Lo que pudiera haber sido una experiencia dura fue una de las mejores temporadas de nuestra vida debido a que una familia tica nos extendió su mano de amistad. Nos ayudaron a descubrir su bello país, a navegar la vida cotidiana, y a practicar español. Sin duda, el mayor aprendizaje de esa etapa vino a través de recibir la hospitalidad cristiana que nos mostraron allí.

A Ponerlo en Práctica
Después de aprender español y vivir en Latinoamérica durante aproximadamente dos años, regresamos a Kansas City con una pasión de demostrarles ese mismo amor y hospitalidad cristiana a los inmigrantes en nuestra ciudad. Nos mudamos a una comunidad con gente de diversos países y empezamos una clase de inglés en nuestra casa. Esa clase fue el comienzo de un nuevo ministerio que se llama Mission Adelante, el cual ha amado y servido a muchos inmigrantes y refugiados de varias naciones desde el 2005.

Un Modelo Relacional
Este currículo, *English Adelante*, es el fruto de nuestras propias experiencias aprendiendo y enseñando otro idioma. Nuestro modelo de enseñanza utiliza a voluntarios que hablan inglés como "compañeros de conversación" y el currículo fue diseñado específicamente para uso en una aula con una proporción de voluntarios a alumnos que se acerca a 1:1. Los beneficios de este método tan individualizado incluyen un énfasis fuerte en la práctica y repetición verbal y la posibilidad de personalizar la experiencia del aprendizaje según la habilidad de cada alumno. Desde el año 2005, un sin fin de voluntarios ha servido, ha enseñado, ha hecho amistad, y ha compartido el amor de Cristo con muchos inmigrantes a través de nuestro programa de inglés. Después de la tabla de contenido, se encuentra el bosquejo que se usa en Mission Adelante para una clase típica de dos horas, durante un curso de 12 semanas.

11 Usos del Verbo "To Be"
El significado de verbo "To Be" en inglés es muy amplio. Es tan poderoso ese verbo, que abarca cinco de los verbos más comunes en español, incluyendo los verbos Ser (soy pastor), Estar (estoy feliz), Hacer (hace frío), Tener (tengo hambre), y Haber (hay comida). Si una persona puede dominar el verbo "To Be", ya está lejos en el camino de hablar inglés. Será evidente que los 11 usos del verbo "To Be" que se enseñan en *English Adelante* representan el inglés más fundamental que se usa en todas las conversaciones cotidianas.

Los Códigos QR y el Audio
Los códigos QR que se encuentran en la primera página de cada lección conecta al alumno con una página del sitio web de Mission Adelante que tiene una guía de audio para *English Adelante* que se puede usar con el currículo para practicar fuera del aula.

Estoy emocionado de poder ofrecer este recurso y le pido a Dios que sea una herramienta útil para individuos y organizaciones que quieren aprender y enseñar inglés con gente de todos lugares.

Sinceramente,
P. Jarrett Meek

table of contents

Author's Note..	3
Standard Class Session Outline...........................	6
Lesson 1: Basics...	7
Lesson 2: Identification...	15
Lesson 3: Characteristics......................................	21
Lesson 4: Time...	27
Lesson 5: Occupation..	33
Lesson 6: Emotion...	41
Lesson 7: Condition..	47
Lesson 8: Progressive Action...............................	53
Lesson 9: Age...	59
Lesson 10: Existence..	65
Lesson 11: Location..	73
Lesson 12: Weather..	79

To access the online audio companion, scan the QR code at the beginning of each lesson with your phone, or visit www.missionadelante.org/english-adelante-audio.

Para acceder el audio, escanee el código QR en el comienzo de cada lección con el celular, o visite www.missionadelante.org/english-adelante-audio.

Standard Class Session Outline

Description: Our Level 1 class is built around 11 uses of the English verb "To Be," and employs volunteer conversation partners in an ideal 1:2 volunteer:student ratio. This ratio maximizes verbal practice, allows for individualization, and fosters the relational dynamics we believe are conducive to language learning.

Conversation Segment 1: Review: 15 Minutes (6:30-6:45)
- As soon as student arrives, partner initiates one-on-one.
- Review conjugation of verb "To Be."
- Review homework, previous vocabulary and uses of the verb "To Be." Focus on having students read their answers aloud.

Instruction Segment 1: Welcome and Review: (6:45-7:00)
The instructor welcomes, prays, and engages the students in relational conversation in a dynamic review of previous lessons and the conjugation of the verb, "To Be." Opening games or activities should launch the class off on a good pace and involve the large group together as well as each person individually.

Instruction Segment 2: Teaching the Response: (7:00-7:10)
Using creative explanation, demonstration and/or activities, the Instructor introduces the main lesson and gives focused instruction on a specific use of the verb, "To Be." Emphasis should be given to the core use in its affirmative and negative forms. Relevant ancillary grammatical issues should not be introduced until later in the session.

Conversation Segment 2: Response Build-up: (7:10-7:30)
- Step 1: New Vocab Repetition: Partner points to a vocab word and says it, the student repeats. Do all the words on the new list.
- Step 2: Sentence Repetition: Partner makes sentences using "To Be" with each vocabulary word, student repeats sentence.
- Step 3: Sentence Formation: Partner gives subject and points to vocab word. Student makes sentence using "To Be" with indicated subject and vocab word.

Instruction Segment 3: Teaching the Key Questions: (7:30-7:45)
Using creative explanation, demonstration and/or activities, the instructor introduces the key questions that address a specific use of the verb "To Be." Other ancillary grammatical issues could be introduced here.

Conversation Segment 3: Combination Segment: (7:45-8:20)
- Step 1: Answering Questions:
  - Using Vocab List: Partner asks the key question and points to a vocab word to indicate the content of the answer. Student answers accordingly using the verb, "To Be."
  - Using Pictures or props: Partner asks the key question and points to a picture or a prop. The student answers the question using the verb, "To Be."
- Step 2: Asking Questions:
  - Using pictures or props: Student asks the key question and points to a picture or prop. The partner answers the question using the verb, "To Be."
- Step 3: Reading and Response
  - This segment can be flexible as well. Work on reading, pronunciation, and responding to a reading could be done. Bible verses, other readings or other conversation activities could be done here.

Closing Segment: (8:20-8:30): Prayer requests, announcements, homework assignments, etc.

Lesson 1
Basics

Lesson 1: Basics
The Verb "To Be"

1. "It <u>is</u> sunny." (weather)

2. "I <u>am</u> from Kansas." (location)

3. There <u>are</u> three." (existence)

4. I <u>am</u> 35 years old." (age)

5. "<u>I'm</u> talking." (progression)

6. "I <u>am</u> cold." (condition)

7. "I <u>am</u> happy." (emotion)

8. "I <u>am</u> a teacher." (occupation)

9. "It <u>is</u> 5 o'clock." (time)

10. "I <u>am</u> tall." (characteristic)

11. "I <u>am</u> James." (identification)

"I am James."

TO BE
(Traducciones al Español)

I <u>am</u> = Yo soy
You <u>are</u> = Tú eres
He (she, it) <u>is</u> = Él/ella es
We <u>are</u> = Nosotros somos
They <u>are</u> = Ellos/ellas son

Lesson 1: Basics
The English Alphabet

Aa	(ei)	**Jj**	(yei)	**Ss**	(es)
Bb	(bi)	**Kk**	(kei)	**Tt**	(ti)
Cc	(si)	**Ll**	(el)	**Uu**	(iu)
Dd	(di)	**Mm**	(em)	**Vv**	(vi)
Ee	(i)	**Nn**	(en)	**Ww**	(dabal iu)
Ff	(ef)	**Oo**	(ou)	**Xx**	(eks)
Gg	(yi)	**Pp**	(pi)	**Yy**	(uai)
Hh	(eich)	**Qq**	(kiu)	**Zz**	(zi)
Ii	(ai)	**Rr**	(ar)		

Subject Pronouns

	Singular	Plural
1st person	I (yo)	we (nosotros)
2nd person	you (tú/usted)	you (ustedes)
3rd person	he (él) she (ella) it (cosa, no persona)	they (ellos/ellas)

Lesson 1: Basics
"To Be" Conjugation

Subject	"To Be"	Contraction
I	am	I'm
you	are	you're
he	is	he's
she	is	she's
it	is	it's
we	are	we're
they	are	they're

Sentence Structure for Statements

subject	+ verb +	descriptive phrase
I	am	a man.
You	are	tall.
He	is	married.
She	is	twenty years old.
It	is	three o'clock.
We	are	very happy.
They	are	doctors.

"It is three o'clock."

Lesson 1: Basics
Question Words

Question word	Translation	Answer
Who?	Quién	a person
What?	Qué	a thing
Which?	Cuál	a thing: limited options
When?	Cuándo	a time
Where?	Dónde	a place
Why?	Por qué	a reason
How?	Cómo	a manner
How many?	Cuántos	a number (count nouns)
How much?	Cuánto	an amount (noncount nouns)

Sentence Structure for Questions

Yes/no question (respuesta sí o no)

verb	+ subject	+ descriptive phrase
Are	you	happy today?
Is	he	young?
Are	they	married?

Other

question word	+ verb	+ descriptive phrase	+ subject
Where	am		I?
When	is		the concert?
Who	is	that beautiful	girl?
Where	is	the interesting	book?

Lesson 1: Basics
Homework

Conjugate the verb "To Be" (is, am, are)

I _____
You _____
He _____
She _____
It _____
We _____
They _____

Write the English word in the blank

esto _____
nombre _____
tío _____
hija _____
por qué _____
tía _____
chica _____
mesa _____

Complete the following sentences using the correct form of the verb "To Be" (am, is, are).
Ejemplo: Jeff __is__ a man.

Maria _____ a little girl.
Harold and Jane _____ parents.
We _____ crazy.
That _____ a house.
Those _____ boys.
You _____ alone.

I _____ a mother.
He _____ my uncle.
Those _____ pencils.
She and I _____ sisters.
_____ we a family?
_____ that a table?

Write the following phrases in English.
Ejemplo: *Su libro (de él)*   **His   book**

Mi lápiz _____
La hermana de ella _____
Los papeles de ellos _____
Tu padre _____

Write the following phrases in English. (*Escribe las siguientes frases en inglés.*)

Este padre _____
Esa mesa _____
Este cuaderno _____
Ese lápiz _____

Esos libros _____
Esa madre _____
Esta silla _____
Estas hermanas _____

Write the pronoun that matches the name. (*Escribe el pronombre que combina con el nombre.*)
Ejemplo: Juan = **he**

Magdalena = _____
Paul and Peter = _____
Thelma and I = _____
The cat = _____
John = _____
David, Kimberly and I = _____

Lesson 1: Basics
Vocabulary Practice

Who?	When?	How?
What?	Where?	How many?
Which?	Why?	How much?

Write the English word next to the Spanish word with the same meaning.

_____ ¿Cuánto?   _____ ¿Cuántos?   _____ ¿Cómo?

_____ ¿Por qué?   _____ ¿Dónde?   _____ ¿Cuando?

_____ ¿Cuál?   _____ ¿Qué?   _____ ¿Quién?

Copy each English vocabulary word three times.

_____   _____   _____   _____
_____   _____   _____   _____
_____   _____   _____   _____

_____   _____   _____   _____
_____   _____   _____   _____
_____   _____   _____   _____

_____   _____   _____   _____
_____   _____   _____   _____
_____   _____   _____   _____

Lesson 2
Identification

Lesson 2: Identification
Concepts

TO BE is used to identify people.
    I am Antonio.
    My name is Antonio.
    He is a boy.
    His name is Alejandro.
    She is a girl.
    Her name is Maria.

TO BE is used to identify things.
    It is a book.
    It is a pencil.
    This is a chair.
    That is a table.

Singular	Plural
this (esto, este, esta)	**these** (estos, estas)
that (eso, ese, esa)	**those** (esos, esas)

Identification: Key Questions

Who are you?
I am James.

Who are they?
They are my friends.

What is it?
It is a book.

What is this?
That is a pencil.

What are these?
Those are shoes.

Identification (con traducción)

- **my** = mi/mis
- **your** = tu/tus
- **his** = su/sus (de él)
- **her** = su/sus (de ella)
- **its** = su/sus (de la cosa)
- **our** = nuestro/nuestros
- **their** = su/sus (de ellos)

Lesson 2: Identification
Vocabulary

LIST 1

father	padre
mother	madre
son	hijo
daughter	hija
husband	esposo
wife	esposa
uncle	tío
aunt	tía
cousin	primo/prima
parents	padres
grandfather	abuelo
grandmother	abuela

LIST 2

pen	pluma/lapicero
pencil	lápiz
chair	silla
table	mesa
book	libro
notebook	cuaderno
homework	tarea
piece of paper	hoja de papel

Identification: Reading

Hello, I'm John. I am a man. I am a husband. I am a father, too. This is my family. My wife's name is Julie. She is a woman. We have four children. I am their father and Julie is their mother.

Our oldest son is Harry. He is a boy. He goes to school. Harry calls me Dad. Our oldest daughter is Sarah. She has a dog. Its name is Sparky. It is a boy. Our youngest son is Gabriel. Gabriel is a boy. Gabriel does not go to school yet. Gabriel is a baby. Our youngest daughter is Michelle. Michelle is also a baby. Michelle and Gabriel are twins.

They are my children. I am their father. We are a happy family.

Lesson 2: Identification
Homework

Conjugate the verb "To Be" (is, am, are)

I	_____
You	_____
He	_____
She	_____
It	_____
We	_____
They	_____
She and I	_____

Write the English word in the blank

padre	_____
madre	_____
hijo	_____
hija	_____
hermano	_____
hermana	_____
lapicero	_____
libro	_____

Complete the following sentences using the correct form of the verb "To Be" (am, is, are).

Ejemplo: Jeff *is* a man.

Shelley _____ a woman.
Harold and Jane _____ babies.
We _____ students.
That _____ a chair.
Those _____ pencils.
You _____ a father.

I _____ a grandfather.
They _____ uncles.
She _____ my daughter.
We _____ cousins.
It _____ a piece of paper.
You _____ a man.

Write the following phrases in English.

Ejemplo: Su libro (de él)   <u>His</u>   <u>book</u>

Mi lápiz _____ _____
La hermana de ella _____ _____
Los cuadernos de ellos _____ _____
Tu madre _____ _____

La madre de nosotros _____ _____
La silla de él. _____ _____
Nuestro abuelo. _____ _____
El hijo de ellos. _____ _____

Write the following phrases in English.

Este padre _____
Esa mesa _____
Este cuaderno _____
Ese lápiz _____

Esa madre _____
Esta silla _____
Esos zapatos _____
Ese libro _____

Write the pronoun that matches the name.

Ejemplo: Juan = **he**

Cristina = _____
Raul and Jaime = _____
Brenda and I = _____
The dog = _____
Peter = _____

Lesson 2: Identification
Vocabulary

father mother son daughter	brother sister husband wife	pen pencil chair table	book notebook piece of paper

Write the English word next to the Spanish word with the same meaning.

_____ esposo   _____ hermana   _____ libro

_____ mesa   _____ madre   _____ hijo

_____ pluma   _____ silla   _____ lápiz

_____ hija   _____ cuaderno   _____ hoja de papel

_____ padre   _____ esposa   _____ hermano

Copy each English vocabulary word three times.

Lesson 3
Characteristics

Lesson 3: Characteristics
Concepts

To be is used to describe the characteristics of people, places, and things.

- I <u>am</u> short.
- You <u>are</u> funny.
- He <u>is</u> tall.
- The book <u>is</u> heavy.
- The pencil <u>is</u> sharp.
- We <u>are</u> intelligent.
- They <u>are</u> pretty.

"I am short."

Characteristics:
Concept

1. **What is _____ like?**
   What is he like?
   He is nice.

2. **What is Mexico like?**
   It is beautiful.

3. **What are you like?**
   I am intelligent.

4. **How would you describe _____?**
   How would you describe Lilia?
   She is very helpful.

5. **How would you describe Brent?**
   He is tall and thin.

6. **How would you describe yourself?**
   I am somewhat talkative.

Traducciones
How would you describe it?
      ¿Cómo lo describiría?

yourself	tú mismo
like	como
kind of	un poco
somewhat	un poco
a little bit	un poquito
very	muy
extremely	sumamente

Lesson 3: Characteristics
Vocabulary

LIST 1	
tall	alto
short	bajo
young	joven
old	viejo
funny	chistoso
serious	serio
noisy	ruidoso
quiet	callado
thin	delgado
fat	gordo
big	grande
small	pequeño
hard	duro
soft	suave
long	largo
short	corto
light	liviano
heavy	pesado

LIST 2	
ugly	feo
fast	rápido
slow	lento
good	bueno
bad	malo
interesting	interesante
boring	aburrido
dark	oscuro
light	claro
intelligent	inteligente
kind	amable
nice	simpático
mean	antipático
married	casado
single	soltero
beautiful	hermoso
pretty	lindo
handsome	guapo

Lesson 3: Characteristics
Dialogue

"**Good morning, I'm John. May I ask you a few questions?**"
    "Yes, you may."
"**Great. What's your name, sir?**"
    "I'm Jackson Smith."
"**Is that J-A-C-K-S-O-N?**"
    "Yes, that's right."
"**Are you married, Jackson?**"
    "No, I'm single."
"**How would you describe yourself?**"
    "Well, I'm tall and thin. I'm very handsome. And I'm extremely intelligent."
"**You are also somewhat proud! Jackson, what is your address?**"
    "My address is 321 Merry Avenue.
"**Thank you, Mr. Smith.**"
    "You're welcome."
"**Have a nice day.**"

Characteristics: Reading

Hello, I'm Mike. I am a very tall man. I'm a husband and a father too. This is my family. My wife's name is Kimberly. She is a beautiful woman. We have four children.

Our oldest son is Isaac. He is strong and very intelligent. He goes to a good school. for Isaac, reading is easier than writing. Our oldest daughter is Avery. She is a kind, young girl. Her hair is long. She is taller than Isaac.

Our youngest son is Ryan. Ryan is a baby boy. He is very small, but he is somewhat fat. He is extremely noisy when he is hungry. Ryan does not go to school yet. Our youngest daughter is Emily. Emily is also a baby. Emily and Ryan are twins, but Emily is smaller than Ryan. She is also much quieter than he is.

They are my beautiful children. I am their father. We are a big, happy family.

Lesson 3: Characteristics
Homework

Conjugate the verb "To Be" (is, am, are)
- I _____
- You _____
- He _____
- She _____
- It _____
- We _____
- They _____

Write the opposite characteristic in the blank
Example: tall   <u>short</u>
- young _____
- funny _____
- talkative _____
- big _____
- hard _____
- long _____
- light _____

Complete the following identification/characteristic sentences using the correct form of the verb "To Be" (am, is, are).
*Ejemplo: Jeff **is** my uncle and he **is** thin.*

Shelley ___ my sister and she _____ beautiful.
Those ____ pennies and each penny _____ small.
This ____ my family and we _____ intelligent.
That woman _____ my teacher and we ____ friends.
Miguel and I _____ brothers and we _____ fast!
I ____ her uncle and she _____ single.

Complete the following sentences using characteristics to describe the subjects given.
*Ejemplo: My mother is **kind**.*

Her pencil is _____.
His aunt is _____.
Their notebooks are _____.
Your mother is _____.

My father is _____.
This class is very _____.
These baseballs are _____.
I am a _____ man.

Use complete sentences and the verb "to be" to answer the following questions.
How would you describe…?   ¿Como describirías…?
Ejemplo: your son? **<u>My son is intelligent.</u>**

your mother? _____.
your father? _____.
a notebook? _____.
a chair? _____.
a piece of paper? _____.

those pencils? _____.
that soccer ball? _____.
your uncle? _____.
yourself? _____.
the President? _____.

Lesson 3: Characteristics
Vocabulary Practice

tall	funny	big	long
short	serious	small	short
young	talkative	hard	light
old	quiet	soft	heavy

Write the English word next to the Spanish word with the same meaning.

_____ chistoso   _____ joven   _____ alto

_____ largo   _____ hablador   _____ serio

_____ liviano   _____ pequeño   _____ callado

_____ bajo   _____ suave   _____ corto

_____ duro   _____ viejo   _____ grande

_____ pesado

Copy each English vocabulary word three times.

26

Lesson 4
Time

Lesson 4: Time
Concepts

The verb, "to be", is used to indicate exact or approximate time.
   *The word "it" is understood to be "the time"
   - It is six o'clock. (6:00) (cuando la hora es exacta se dice "o'clock.")
   - It is *about* six-thirty. (6:29)
   - It is five o'clock in the morning. (La frase, "in the morning", "in the evening" o "at night" se puede usar para clarificar a.m. o p.m.)

The verb, "to be", is used to describe relative time and general time of day.
   - It is early.
   - It is late.
   - It is morning.
   - It is night time.

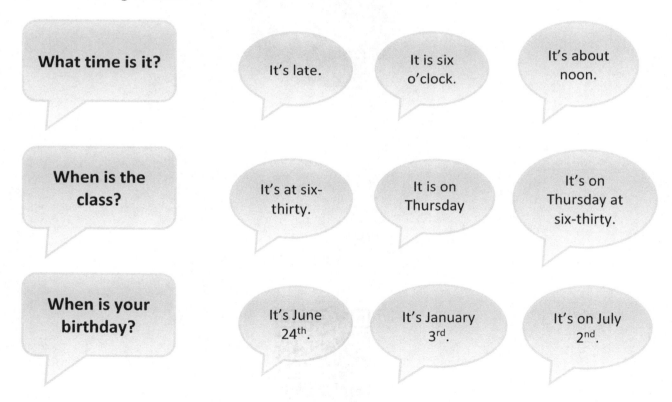

What time is it?	It's late.	It is six o'clock.	It's about noon.
When is the class?	It's at six-thirty.	It is on Thursday	It's on Thursday at six-thirty.
When is your birthday?	It's June 24th.	It's January 3rd.	It's on July 2nd.

Lesson 4: Time
Vocabulary

LIST 1

noon	mediodía
midnight	medianoche
morning	mañana
afternoon	tarde (12:00 – 6:00 p.m.)
evening	tarde (6:00 – 9:00 p.m.)
night	noche
early	temprano
late	tarde
about	aproximadamente
o'clock	se usa para describir la hora
'til or until	indica que faltan minutos para la hora
today	hoy
tomorrow	mañana
yesterday	ayer
next	la próxima
last	la última

LIST 2

Sunday	domingo
Monday	lunes
Tuesday	martes
Wednesday	miércoles
Thursday	jueves
Friday	viernes
Saturday	sábado
January	enero
February	febrero
March	marzo
April	abril
May	mayo
June	junio
July	julio
August	agosto
September	septiembre
October	octubre
November	noviembre
December	diciembre

Lesson 4: Time
Homework

Conjugate the verb "To Be" (is, am, are)

I _____
You _____
He _____
She _____
It _____
We _____
They _____

Write the time in long form using o'clock.

6:00   six o'clock
7:00   _____
9:00   _____
1:00   _____
4:00   _____
2:00   _____
8:00   _____
12:00   _____
10:00   _____
3:00   _____

Complete the following sentences using the correct form of the verb "to be" (am, is, are).
*Ejemplo: The dog **is** hungry, it **is** twelve o'clock.*

Oh no, I _____ late, it _____ nine o'clock!
Tim and Bob _____ home and it _____ two o'clock.
He _____ done, it _____ five o'clock.
Jenny and I _____ hungry because it _____ one o'clock.
She _____ sick and it _____ only twelve o'clock.
They _____ late, it _____ already eleven o'clock!

Complete the following sentences using the verb "to be" and specific times.
*Ejemplo: The class **is at five o'clock**.*

The show _____.
Dinner _____.
Breakfast _____.
Bedtime _____.
The soccer match _____.
Her last class _____.
His dentist appointment _____.
News _____.

Use complete sentences and the verb "to be" to answer the following questions.
*Ejemplo: When is your birthday? **My birthday is June 25**.*

When is your birthday? My birthday _____.
When is Christmas? _____.
When is the exam? _____.
What time is the class? _____.
What time is it? _____.

Lesson 4: Time
Vocabulary Practice

today tomorrow yesterday Sunday Monday Tuesday	Wednesday Thursday Friday Saturday	January February March April May	June July August September October	November December

Write the English word next to the Spanish word with the same meaning.

_____ junio _____ miércoles _____ martes
_____ febrero _____ domingo _____ mañana
_____ julio _____ marzo _____ viernes
_____ mayo _____ sábado _____ lunes
_____ octubre _____ hoy _____ septiembre
_____ abril _____ enero _____ diciembre
_____ noviembre _____ ayer _____ agosto
_____ jueves

Copy each English vocabulary word three times.

Lesson 5
Occupation

Lesson 5: Occupation
Concept

The verb, "to be", is used to describe occupations.
- I am a doctor.
- You are a receptionist.
- She is a teacher.
- He is a carpenter.
- They are landscapers.
    (la "a" sólo se usa cuando el sujeto es singular.)

The verb, "to work", is used to describe a place or field of work.
- You work in a factory.
- They work in construction.

To Work (trabajar)
I work
you work
he/she/it works
we work
they work

The verb, "to do", is used to ask questions about occupation.
- What do you do?
- Where do you work?
- Do you work?

The verb, "to do", is used to create negative sentences.
- I do *not* work.

The verb, "to do", is used to add emphasis or clarification.
- I *do* work!

To Do (hacer)
I do
you do
he/she/it does
we do
they do

Lesson 5: Occupation
Key Questions

What do you do?
    I am a waitress.
    I work in a restaurant.

What is his job?
    He is a doctor.
    He is a teacher.

What kind of work do they do?
    They are plumbers.
    They are landscapers.
    They are bus drivers.

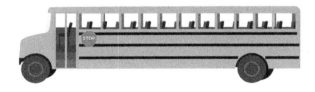

Lesson 5: Occupation
Vocabulary

LIST 1

plumber	plomero
cook	cocinero
server	mesero
cashier	cajero
doctor	doctor
nurse	enfermera
teacher	maestro
student	estudiante
mechanic	mecánico
manager	gerente
landscaper	jardinero
housekeeper	ama de llaves
homemaker	ama de casa
bus driver	chofer
lawyer	abogado
electrician	electricista
receptionist	recepcionista
pastor	pastor
roofer	techero
carpenter	carpintero
factory worker	trabajador de fábrica
construction worker	constructor

LIST 2

restaurant	restaurante
supermarket	supermercado
hospital	hospital
school	escuela
auto shop	taller mecánico
office	oficina
hotel	hotel
post office	correo
bank	banco
parking lot	estacionamiento
supply room	almacén
hall	corredor, pasillo
meeting room	sala de juntas

Lesson 5: Occupation
Reading

Hello, I'm John. I am a very tall man. I'm a carpenter. I work on houses. My wife's name is Julie. She is a beautiful woman. Julie works at a school. She is a teacher. She is a very good teacher. She is a good mother, too. We have four children.

Our oldest son is Harry. He's strong and very intelligent. He goes to a good school. Harry is a student. Our oldest daughter is Sarah. She is a kind young girl. Her hair is long. She is taller than Harry. She is a student, too. She is a good student.

Gabriel is a baby boy. He is very small, but he is somewhat fat. He is extremely noisy when he is hungry. Gabriel does not go to school yet. Our youngest daughter is Michelle. She is also a baby. Michelle and Gabriel are twins, but Michelle is smaller than Gabriel.

We are a big, happy family.

Lesson 5: Occupation
Homework

Conjugate the verb "To Be" (is, am, are)

I _____	You and I _____	Yes, it _____.
You _____	He and I _____	I _____ old but they _____ not.
She _____	It is true that I _____	_____ we?
It _____	That _____	She _____ late.
We _____	These _____	Those _____.
They _____	This _____	_____ I?

Write the English word in the blank and then say it aloud.

plomero	_____	supermercado	_____
cocinero	_____	banco	_____
mesero	_____	sala de juntas	_____
cajero	_____	pastor	_____
doctor	_____	abogado	_____
enfermera	_____	chofer	_____
maestro	_____	almacén	_____
gerente	_____	taller mecánico	_____
jardinero	_____	recepcionista	_____
ama de llaves	_____	electricista	_____

Complete the following sentences using the correct form of the verb "To Be" (am, is, are).
Ejemplo: He <u>is</u> a cook. They <u>are</u> cooks.

John _____ a doctor.   Sara and Ann _____ cooks.
I _____ a pastor.   They _____ good servers.
We _____ students.   He _____ a plumber.
You _____ a teacher.   Alejandro and I _____ excellent landscapers.
They _____ nurses.   I _____ a roofer every Saturday.
She _____ a receptionist.   We _____ professional carpenters.

Complete the following sentences using the verb "to be" and occupations.
Ejemplo: My uncles. <u>They are doctors</u> o <u>My uncles are doctors</u>.

My father _____.
Your brothers _____.
Your sister _____.
You _____.

Use complete sentences and the verb "to be" to answer the following questions.
Ejemplo: What does your uncle do? <u>He is a mechanic</u> o <u>My uncle is a mechanic.</u>

What does your father do? My father is_____.
What does your neighbor do? _____.
What do you do? _____.

Lesson 5: Occupation
Vocabulary Practice

plumber	doctor	mechanic
cook	nurse	manager
server	teacher	landscaper
cashier	student	housekeeper

Write the English word next to the Spanish word with the same meaning.

_____ maestro _____ cajero _____ ama de llaves

_____ mecánico _____ gerente _____ plomero

_____ estudiante _____ jardinero _____ cocinero

_____ mesero _____ doctor _____ enfermera

Copy each English vocabulary word three times.

Lesson 6
Emotion

Lesson 6: Emotion
Concept

The verb, "to be", "to feel", and "to seem" are used to express an emotional state:

I <u>am</u> happy.

He <u>feels</u> embarrassed.

We're in love.

You <u>seem</u> sad today.

She <u>seems</u> nervous.

They <u>feel</u> angry.

To Feel (sentirse)		**To Seem** (parecer)	
I	**feel**	I	**seem**
you	**feel**	you	**seem**
he/she/it	**feels**	he/she/it	**seems**
we	**feel**	we	**seem**
they	**feel**	they	**seem**

Lesson 6: Emotion
Key Questions and Vocabulary

How are you?
    I'm fine, thank you.
    I feel discouraged.
    I'm kind of sad.

How is he doing?
    He's pretty sad about his grandma's death.
    He seems okay.

How do you feel?
    I'm very happy.

LIST 1
today *(hoy)*
now *(ahora)*
very *(muy)*
pretty *(muy – menos fuerte)*
a little *(un poco)*
a little bit *(un poquito)*
kind of *(más o menos)*
about *(acerca de)*
because *(porque)*

LIST 2
happy	contento
sad	triste
angry	enojado
fine	bien
excited	emocionado
disappointed	decepcionado
embarrassed	avergonzado
frustrated	frustrado
worried	preocupado
encouraged	animado
discouraged	desanimado
depressed	deprimido
down	triste

LIST 3
well	bien
proud	tener orgullo
irritated	molesto
furious	furioso
satisfied	satisfecho
delighted	encantado
in love	enamorado
peaceful	tranquilo
disturbed	perturbado
desperate	desesperado
safe	seguro
afraid	con miedo

Lesson 6: Emotion
Reading

Hello, I'm John and this is my wife, Julie. We are very excited today because our son Harry has passed his reading test. I am very proud of Harry because he has worked very hard. Harry is very happy.

Our daughter Sarah is not very happy. She feels down because she did not pass her reading test. She is worried because she thinks we are angry with her. I am not angry. I feel sad for her. My wife is a little embarrassed because Gabriel and Michelle are crying in the grocery store. She is irritated. She does not feel peaceful right now. She feels frustrated.

We are a happy family, but sometimes life is hard.

Lesson 6: Emotion
Homework

Conjugate the verb "To Be" (is, am, are) and then say it aloud.

I _____	You _____	She _____
We _____	They _____	I _____
He _____	We _____	You _____
They _____	I _____	We _____
It _____	She _____	It _____
You _____	He _____	They _____

Write the English word in the blank and then say it aloud.

nervioso _____	furioso _____
bien _____	perturbado _____
emocionado _____	con miedo _____
triste _____	decepcionado _____
contento _____	más o menos _____
animado _____	avergonzado _____
frustrado _____	encantado _____
enojado _____	molesto _____
preocupado _____	deprimido _____

Complete the following sentences using the correct form of the verb "To Be" and then, "To feel" (am, is, are, feel, feels) in the other column.

Ejemplo: He <u>is</u> happy. *Ejemplo*: They <u>feel</u> peaceful.

We _____ angry.   We _____ angry.
They _____ happy.   They _____ happy.
You _____ a little worried.   You _____ a little worried.
Amy _____ discouraged.   Amy _____ discouraged.
She _____ furious.   She _____ furious.

Complete the following sentences using the verb "to be" or "to feel" and an emotion.

Ejemplo: They _____. They <u>are</u> very <u>angry</u>. My sister _____. My sister <u>feels</u> a little <u>sad.</u>

My son _____.
Your daughters_____.
You _____.
I _____.

Use complete sentences and the verb "to be" or "to feel" to answer the following questions.

Ejemplo: *How is your brother?* He <u>is</u> kind of <u>sad</u> today.

How is your mother? She feels _____.
How are your friends today? _____.
How are you doing? _____.
How is your daughter today? _____.

Lesson 6: Emotion
Vocabulary Practice

happy	excited	frustrated
sad	disappointed	worried
angry	embarrassed	encouraged
fine	nervous	discouraged

Write the English word next to the Spanish word with the same meaning.

_____ avergonzado   _____ nervioso   _____ triste
_____ desanimado   _____ emocionado   _____ preocupado
_____ enojado   _____ contento   _____ animado
_____ frustrado   _____ bien   _____ decepcionado

Copy each English vocabulary word three times.

Lesson 7
Condition

Lesson 7: Condition
Concept

The verbs, "to be" and "to feel", are used to express temporary conditions of <u>people</u>.
- I <u>am</u> tired.
- He<u>'s</u> hungry.
- She<u>'s</u> awake.
- We <u>feel</u> sick.
- They <u>feel</u> cold.

"To be" is used to express temporary conditions of <u>things.</u>
- The glass <u>is</u> empty.
- The plates <u>are</u> clean.
  *In English, adjectives have no plural form. You would not say, "The plates are clean<u>s</u>."
- The coffee <u>is not</u> very hot.
  *In English, the word "not" indicates negativity of a statement. It comes after the verb.

Condition:
Key Questions

How are you?
  I'm cold.
  I'm very hungry.
  I feel energetic.

How is he doing?
  He's sick.
  He feels very tired.

How would you describe the pencil?
  It's broken.
  It's sharp.

Lesson 7: Condition
Vocabulary

LIST 1

plumber	plomero
cook	cocinero
tired	cansado
rested	descansado
cold	con frío
hot	con calor/caliente
hungry	con hambre
satisfied	satisfecho
sick	enfermo
healthy	sano/saludable
full	lleno
empty	vacío
clean	limpio
dirty	sucio
old	viejo
new	nuevo
open	abierto
closed	cerrado
sleepy	con sueño
asleep	dormido
awake	despierto
well	sano

LIST 2

energetic	con energía
strong	fuerte
weak	débil
ready	listo
married	casado
single	soltero
broken	roto, quebrado, descompuesto
torn	roto – papel o tela
fixed	arreglado
alive	vivo
dead	muerto
on	encendido, prendido
off	apagado
comfortable	cómodo
uncomfortable	incómodo
wet	mojado
dry	seco

Lesson 7: Condition
Reading

Hello, I'm John and this is my wife, Julie. We are tired and cold today. We are not very well-rested. Our house is cold. The heater is old and dirty. It is not on. It's broken.

We are ready for dinner. I am very hungry. Our children are hungry too. The food is on the table and it is hot. We are ready to eat. Gabriel and Michelle are asleep. The light in the room is off. They are in their beds, but Harry and Sarah are awake. They are all cold, but they are not sick. They are young and strong.

We are uncomfortable, but at least we're healthy.

Lesson 7: Condition
Homework

Conjugate the verb "To Be" (is, am, are), then, say it aloud.

I _____	You _____	She _____
We _____	They _____	I _____
He _____	We _____	You _____
She _____	It _____	He _____
They _____	I _____	We _____
It _____	She _____	It _____
You _____	He _____	They _____

Write the English word in the blank and then say it aloud.

cansado	_____	saludable	_____
enfermo	_____	vacío	_____
frío	_____	fuerte	_____
con hambre	_____	soltero	_____
lleno	_____	cómodo	_____
viejo	_____	muerto	_____
sucio	_____	seco	_____
nuevo	_____	quebrado	_____
limpio	_____	con sueño	_____

Complete the following sentences using the correct form of the verb "To Be" or "To feel" (am, is, are, feel, feels) and then say it aloud.

Ejemplo: He <u>is</u> happy. They <u>feel</u> peaceful.

The table _____ dirty.   We _____ not well rested.
The children _____ hungry.   The heater _____ old and dirty.
We _____ a little tired.   Our house _____ cold.
The cup _____ full.   The light in their room _____ off.

Complete the following sentences using the verb "to be" or "to feel" and conditions.

Ejemplo: Your sister _____. She <u>**is very weak**</u>. O My sister <u>**feels energetic.**</u>

His daughter _____.
Your friend _____.
We _____.
The house _____.

Use complete sentences and the verb "to be" or "to feel" to answer the following questions.

Ejemplo: He <u>feels</u> sick today.

How are your brothers? They feel _____.
How is your grandmother? _____.
How are you doing? _____.
How is your daughter today? _____.

Lesson 7: Condition
Vocabulary Practice

tired	hungry	full	old
rested	satisfied	empty	new
cold	sick	clean	
hot	healthy	dirty	

Write the English word next to the Spanish word with the same meaning.

_____ lleno _____ enfermo _____ con calor
_____ con hambre _____ vacío _____ descansado
_____ sucio _____ cansado _____ satisfecho
_____ saludable _____ limpio _____ nuevo
_____ con frío _____ viejo

Copy each English vocabulary word three times.

52

Lesson 8
Progressive Action

Lesson 8: Progressive Action
Concept

The verb, "to be", is used with another verb to indicate an action in progress. The suffix "ing" is added to the end of the verb to indicate progressive action.

To be + gerund   =   Estar + gerundio

I am read**ing**.   Estoy le**yendo**.
You are writ**ing**.   Estás escrib**iendo**.
He is eat**ing**.   Él está com**iendo**.
The book is fall**ing**.   El libro está ca**yendo**.
We are study**ing**.   Estamos estudi**ando**.
The children are play**ing**. Los niños están jug**ando**.

Lesson 8: Progressive Action
Key Questions

What are you doing?
    I am cooking.
    I'm working.
    We are walking.

What's going on? (informal)
    I'm studying.
    We're cleaning.
    They are eating.
    They're playing.

Lesson 8: Progressive Action
Vocabulary

LIST 1

to talk (talking)	hablar
to listen (listening)	escuchar
to read (reading)	leer
to write (writing)	escribir
to go (going)	ir (yendo)
to do (doing)	hacer
to cook (cooking)	cocinar
to eat (eating)	comer
to clean (cleaning)	limpiar
to sleep (sleeping)	dormir
to walk (walking)	caminar
to play (playing)	jugar
to fall (falling)	caer
to study (studying)	estudiar
to drink (drinking)	beber o tomar
to wear (wearing)	llevar (ropa)
to run (running)	correr
to see (seeing)	ver

LIST 2

to grab (grabbing)	agarrar
to throw (throwing)	lanzar/tirar
to come (coming)	venir
to leave (leaving)	salir
to touch (touching)	tocar
to ask (asking)	preguntar
to answer (answering)	contestar
to ask for (asking)	pedir
to pray (praying)	orar/rezar
to help (helping)	ayudar
to watch (watching)	mirar
to give (giving)	dar
to drive (driving)	conducir

Lesson 8: Progressive Action
Homework

Conjugate the verb "To Be" (is, am, are), then, say it aloud.

I _____	You _____	She _____
We _____	They _____	I _____
He _____	We _____	You _____
She _____	It _____	He _____
They _____	I _____	We _____
It _____	She _____	It _____
You _____	He _____	They _____

Write the English gerund (progressive action) in the blank.
Ejemplo: dormir   **Sleeping**

caminar	_____	ir	_____
escuchar	_____	manejar	_____
comer	_____	preguntar	_____
hablar	_____	mirar	_____
limpiar	_____	estudiar	_____
leer	_____	correr	_____
escribir	_____	jugar	_____

Complete the following sentences using the correct form of the verb "To Be" (am, is, are).
Ejemplo: He **is** cooking the chicken. They **are** driving the car.

The president _____ talking to him.   He and I _____ walking by the river.
The boys _____ playing soccer.   Mary _____ reading the book.
We _____ writing a book.   They _____ coming at 2 o'clock.
The men _____ working on the road.   I _____ grabbing the ball.
I _____ eating a hamburger.   Claudia _____ doing homework.

Complete the following sentences using the verb "to be" and a gerund to indicate progressive action.
Ejemplo: They _____. They **are praying**.

My sister _____.   We _____.
Your wife _____.   His daughter _____.
Those children _____.   It _____.
Tom and John _____.   Tony and I _____.

Use complete sentences and the verb "to be" with the gerund to answer the following questions indicating progression.
Ejemplo: What is he doing? He **is playing** futbol.

What are you doing? _____.
What is your family doing? _____.
What are we doing? _____.
What is your husband doing? _____.

57

Lesson 8: Progressive Action Vocabulary Practice

to talk	to go	to clean
to listen	to do	to sleep
to read	to cook	to walk
to write	to eat	to play

Write the English word next to the Spanish word with the same meaning.

_____ cocinar   _____ hacer   _____ limpiar
_____ leer   _____ comer   _____ escuchar
_____ ir   _____ hablar   _____ jugar
_____ escribir _____ dormir   _____ caminar

Copy each English vocabulary word three times.

Lesson 9
Age

Lesson 9: Age
Concept

The verb, "to be" is used to express the age of people in years, months, weeks, or days.

- I am 35 years old.
- Brent's grandma is 100 years old.
- My son is 5 weeks old.
- These infants are only 2 days old.

"To be" is used to express the age of things, buildings, businesses, etc.

- This building is at least 80 years old.
- These pictures of my mother are more than 50 years old.
- Our family business is a century old.

Lesson 9: Age
Key Questions

How old are you?
I'm 35 years old.

How old is your son?
He's 3 weeks old.

How old are these books?
They're at least 100 years old.

About how old is this building?
It's about 80 years old.

How old is the United States?
It's more than 2 centuries old.

Age:
Vocabulary

day	*día*	1	one	16	sixteen
week	*semana*	2	two	17	seventeen
month	*mes*	3	three	18	eighteen
year	*año*	4	four	19	nineteen
decade	*década*	5	five	20	twenty
century	*siglo*	6	six	30	thirty
and a half	*y medio*	7	seven	40	forty
almost	*casi*	8	eight	50	fifty
about	*a cerca de*	9	nine	60	sixty
nearly	*casi*	10	ten	70	seventy
at least	*por lo menos*	11	eleven	80	eighty
more than	*más que*	12	twelve	90	ninety
approximately	*aproximadamente*	13	thirteen	100	one hundred
		14	fourteen	1,000	one thousand
		15	fifteen		

Lesson 9: Age
Reading

Hello, I'm John. I'm a husband and a father, but I am still a young man. I am thirty-eight years old. My wife Julie is a mother, but she is still young and beautiful. She's thirty-two.

Harry is our oldest son. He is fifteen years old. He's a student. He wants to be a doctor. Peter drives an old car. It is more than fifteen years old. Lauren is also a student. She is thirteen. Harold and Jane are our twin babies. They are only three and a half weeks old.

We live in an old house. It is at least a century old. That's one hundred years! Old houses are beautiful, but they need a lot of work.

Lesson 9: Age
Homework

Conjugate the verb "To Feel" (feel, feels), then, say it aloud.

I _____	You _____	She _____
We _____	They _____	I _____
He _____	We _____	You _____
She _____	It _____	He _____
They _____	I _____	We _____
It _____	She _____	It _____
You _____	He _____	They _____

Write the English word in the blank.

año	_____	negocio	_____
mes	_____	y medio	_____
semana	_____	catorce	_____
día	_____	cien	_____
viejo	_____	aproximadamente	_____
casi	_____	once	_____
por lo menos	_____	edificio	_____
más que	_____	mil	_____

Complete the following sentences using the correct form of the verb "To Be" (am, is, are).

Ejemplo: He *is* five years old. They **are** at least 20 years old.

The teacher _____ about 30 years old.   He _____ almost 10 years old.
The girls _____ 15 years old.   That movie _____ approximately 5 years old.
We _____ more than 25 years old.   They _____ living in a house that is 2 years old.
My father _____ at least 60 years old.   Claudia _____ 10 and a half years old.
I _____ 35 years old.   That book _____ almost a century old.
The school _____ about 35 years old.   I _____ feeling like I _____ 90 years old today.

Complete the following sentences using the verb "to be" to indicate age.

Ejemplo: They **are 15 years old** o My sister **is about 25 years old.**

My son _____.
Your husband _____.
We _____.
The picture _____.

Use complete sentences and the verb "to be" to answer the following questions indicating ages.

Ejemplo: How old is your uncle? **He is 30 years old**.

How old is your father? He is _____.
How old are these pictures? _____.
How old are your children? _____.
About how old is your house? _____.

Lesson 9: Age
Vocabulary Practice

Write the number in word form next to each number.

1 ___One___	11 _____	20 _____
2 _____	12 _____	30 _____
3 _____	13 _____	40 _____
4 _____	14 _____	50 _____
5 _____	15 _____	60 _____
6 _____	16 _____	70 _____
7 _____	17 _____	80 _____
8 _____	18 _____	90 _____
9 _____	19 _____	100 _____
10 _____		1000 _____

Write the English word next to the Spanish word with the same meaning.

house car building	business photo movie

_____ foto   _____ película
_____ edificio   _____ negocio
_____ casa   _____ carro

Copy each English vocabulary word three times.

_____ _____ _____ _____
_____ _____ _____ _____
_____ _____ _____ _____

_____ _____
_____ _____
_____ _____

Lesson 10
Existence

Lesson 10: Existence
Concept

The verb, "to be" is used to state the existence of people or things.
- There is a car.
- There is a God.
- There are three policemen.
- There are five cookies.
  *La "a" sólo se usa con el singular.

The location of the person or object is usually indicated along with the statement of existence.

- There is a car in the driveway.
- There are four policemen at our house.
- There are at least seven cookies on your plate.
- There is a ball under the table.

Lesson 10: Existence
Key Questions

Is there a doctor here?
    Yes, there is a doctor here.
    Yes, there are two doctors here.

Is there a tree in your yard?
    Yes, there is a tree in my yard.

Are there any leaves in your yard?
    Yes, there are leaves in my yard.

How many people are there at this table?
    There are six people at this table.

there	*(hay) Se usa con "to be" para expresar existencia.*
any	*(algún, algunos) Se usa con preguntas.*
some	*(algún, algunos, unos) Se usa con afirmaciones.*
not any	*(ningún, ninguno)*
none	*(ningún, ninguno)*
almost	*(casi)*
about	*(cerca de)*
nearly	*(cerca de)*
at least	*(por lo menos)*
more than	*(más que)*
approximately	*(aproximadamente)*

Lesson 10: Existence
Vocabulary

LIST 1

plate	plato
bowl	plato hondo, tazón
glass	vaso
fork	tenedor
spoon	cuchara
knife	cuchillo
napkin	servilleta
grape	uva
apple	manzana
banana	plátano
strawberry	fresa
cookie	galleta
chip	chip
cake	pastel
candle	vela

LIST 2

food	comida
cheese	queso
fruit	fruta
vegetable	verdura
meat	carne
chicken	pollo
fish	pescado
milk	leche
coffee	café
juice	jugo
ice cream	helado

Lesson 10: Existence
Reading

Hello, I'm John. My wife's name is Julie. There are four children in our family. Their names are Harry, Sarah, Gabriel and Michelle. There are two girls. There are two boys. There are six of us all together.

Julie is a good cook. It is time for dinner. There are many things on the table. There are six plates on the table. There are also six glasses. There are forks and spoons on the table too. There are napkins under the forks. There are many things in the kitchen. There are pots and pans. There is milk in the refrigerator. There are at least ten cookies in the cookie jar. There is flour and there is sugar in the cabinet. There is a mess on the floor too!

Lesson 10: Existence
Homework

Conjugate the verb "To be" (is, am, are), then, say it aloud.

I _____	You _____	She _____
We _____	They _____	I _____
He _____	We _____	You _____
She _____	It _____	He _____
They _____	I _____	We _____
It _____	She _____	It _____
You _____	He _____	They _____

Write the English word in the blank.

cuchillo _____	vela _____
vaso _____	tazón _____
tenedor _____	uva _____
plato _____	pollo _____
servilleta _____	leche _____
galleta _____	jugo _____
pastel _____	por lo menos _____

Complete the following sentences using the correct form of the verb "To Be" (am, is, are).

Ejemplo: There *is* a boy. *Is* there tree?

There _____ a man.   There _____ at least 3 questions.
There _____ 3 plates.   There _____ almost 20 people here.
There _____ doctors.   There _____ one person in my house.
There _____ 4 bedrooms and 2 bathrooms.   _____ there one car in the garage?
There _____ a notebook.   There _____ 2 dozen tacos.
There _____ a pencil.   _____ there any meat?

Complete the following sentences using "There" and the verb "to be" to indicate existence.

Ejemplo: **There are** 4 cookies. **There is** a chair.

_____ a house.   _____ six candles.
_____ many students.   _____ grapes.
_____ a river.   _____ one plate.
_____ some mountains.   _____ 5 knives.

Use "There" and the verb "to be" to answer the following questions indicating existence.

Ejemplo: Are there any pictures? **Yes, there are** 4 pictures. O **No, there are not** any pictures.

Are there any chips? Yes, _____.
Is there any cheese? _____.
How many forks are there? _____.
Are there any children here? _____.
Is there a notebook on the floor? _____.

Lesson 10: Existence
Vocabulary

plate	spoon	banana
bowl	knife	cookie
glass	napkin	chip
fork	apple	cake

Write the English word next to the Spanish word with the same meaning.

_____ tenedor _____ plátano _____ cuchillo
_____ manzana _____ plato _____ chip
_____ galleta _____ cuchara _____ vaso
_____ plato hondo _____ servilleta _____ pastel

Copy each English vocabulary word three times.

71

72

Lesson 11
Location

Lesson 11: Location
Concept

The verb, "to be" is used to describe the location of people and things in relation to the person speaking.
- I am **here**.
- You are **there**.
- The ball is **over there**.
- The children are **way over there**.

The verb, "to be" is used to describe the location of people and things in relation to another person, place, or object.
- I am **inside** the house.
- You are **on** a chair.
- The ball is **under** the table.
- She is **on** the couch.
- We are **near** Missouri.
- The clouds are **above** our heads.

Location:
Key Questions

Where are you?
I'm in the kitchen.
I'm over here.
I'm in Kansas City.

Where is the book?
It's over here.
It's over there.
It's way over there.
It's on the table.
It's in my bag.

Where are you from?
I am from Ciudad Juarez.
I am from Chihuahua.
I am from Mexico.

Lesson 11: Location
Vocabulary

LIST 1		LIST 2	
right here	aquí mismo	**kitchen**	cocina
here	aquí	**bathroom**	baño
over here	acá, por acá	**dining room**	comedor
right there	allí mismo	**living room**	sala
there	allí	**bedroom**	recámara
over there	por allí	**basement**	sótano
way over there	allá	**floor**	piso
on the right	a la derecha	**wall**	pared
on the left	a la izquierda	**ceiling**	techo de adentro
on	encima de	**roof**	techo de afuera
on top of	encima de, sobre	**cabinet**	gabinete
over	arriba de	**refrigerator**	refrigerador
in	en	**closet**	ropero, armario
under	debajo de	**shelf**	repisa
inside	en, adentro de	**box**	caja
outside	afuera de	**bag**	bolsa
beside	al lado de	**city**	ciudad
between	entre	**state**	estado
across from	enfrente de	**country (USA)**	país (EEUU)
in front of	delante de	**country (farm)**	campo
behind	detrás de		

Lesson 11: Location
Reading

Hello, I'm John. I am a very tall man. I'm a carpenter. I am from Mexico. My wife's name is Julie. She is a beautiful woman. Julie works at a school. She is a teacher. She is a very good teacher. She is a good mother too. Julie is from California. We live in Kansas City. We are in the city, not in the country. Our house is on 18th Street. It is a small house, but it is pretty.

I am at work. I am on the roof of a very tall house. My car is in front of the house, on the street. I am very close to my home. It is right over there, to the east. My wife is at home with our two babies. Gabriel and Michelle are both in bed. Their bedroom is at the end of the hall on the left. Julie is in the kitchen. The meat is in a pot on the stove. There is water in the pot too. Harry and Sarah are still at school.

Lesson 11: Location
Homework

Conjugate the verb "To be" (is, am, are), then, say it aloud.

I _____	You _____	She _____
We _____	They _____	I _____
He _____	We _____	You _____
She _____	It _____	He _____
They _____	I _____	We _____

Write the English word in the blank

en _____
debajo de _____
encima de _____
aquí _____
allí _____
allá _____
detrás de _____
sobre _____
dentro de _____
entre _____

Complete the following sentences using the correct form of the verb "To Be" (am, is, are).
Ejemplo: He *is* in the house.

Elena _____ at work.
I _____ over here.
We _____ in the classroom.
You _____ under the bed.
They _____ in Mexico.
She _____ between John and James.

Complete the following sentences using the verb "to be" and a location.
Ejemplo: They *are at work*. John *is over here*.

My father _____.
Your brothers _____.
You _____.
I _____.

Use complete sentences and the verb "to be" to answer the following questions.
Ejemplo: Where is the pencil? **It is on the table.**

Where is the book? It is _____.
Where are your children? _____.
Where is your notebook? _____.
Where are you? _____.

Lesson 11: Location
Vocabulary Practice

right here	there	on top of	under	between
here	over there	over	inside	across from
over here	way over there	above	outside	in front of
right there	on	in	beside	behind

Write the English word next to the Spanish word with the same meaning.

_____ sobre
_____ acá, por acá
_____ debajo de
_____ entre
_____ allí mismo
_____ al lado de
_____ arriba de

_____ por allí
_____ en
_____ enfrente de
_____ aquí
_____ detrás de
_____ arriba de
_____ allá

_____ aquí mismo
_____ afuera de
_____ encima de
_____ delante de
_____ allá
_____ en, dentro de

Copy each English vocabulary word three times.

78

Lesson 12
Weather

Lesson 12: Weather
Concept

The verb, "to be" is used to describe the weather.
- It is cold.
- It is windy out today.
- It's sunny and warm outside.
- The weather is nice today.

The verb, "to be" is used to describe the general climate in a region of specific area or during a season.
- It is normally rainy in Washington State.
- The climate in Arizona is hot and dry.
- In Kansas, it is very cold in the winter time.
- It's snowy and cold in the mountains.

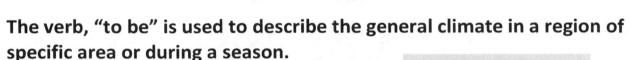

Weather: Key Questions

What's the weather like today?
　It's cloudy and cold.

How is the weather today?
　It's sunny and warm.

What's the temperature like?
　It's warm out today.

What's the weather like in Kansas during the winter?
　It's cold and snowy.

What's like the climate like in Mexico?
　It's hot and dry.

it	se refiere al tiempo de hoy o al clima en general
out	afuera
outside	afuera
like	como (¿Cómo es...?)
very	mucho
a little	un poco
extremely	muchísimo
better	mejor
worse	peor
during	durante

Lesson 12: Weather
Vocabulary

LIST 1

weather	tiempo, clima
climate	clima general de un área
spring	primavera
summer	verano
fall	otoño
winter	invierno
It's cold.	Hace frío.
It's cool.	Está fresco.
It's warm.	Hace poco calor.
It's hot.	Hace calor.
It's sunny.	Hace sol.
It's raining.	Está lloviendo.
It's cloudy.	Está nublado.
It's windy.	Hace viento.
It's snowing.	Está nevando.

LIST 2

It's nice.	Está agradable.
It's freezing.	Hace muchísimo frío.
It's muggy.	Hace calor y está húmedo.
It's sprinkling.	Está lloviendo poquito.
It's pouring.	Está lloviendo fuerte.
It's foggy.	Hay neblina.
It's dry.	Está seco.
It's damp.	Está húmedo y fresco.
It's raining cats and dogs.	Está lloviendo a cántaros.

Lesson 12: Weather
Reading

It's November in Kansas. It is fall. In the fall, the leaves fall from the trees. When it is windy, the leaves blow all around. The weather is warm on some days and cold on others. It often rains in the fall in Kansas and sometimes it snows. Today it is cloudy outside, but it isn't rainy or snowy. It's pretty cold, but December will be colder.

During the spring and summer, the weather is usually sunny and warm. Sometimes it is too hot and sunny. But hot is better than cold!

Lesson 12: Weather
Homework

Conjugate the verb "To be" (is, am, are), then, say it aloud.

I _____	You _____	She _____
We _____	They _____	I _____
He _____	We _____	You _____
She _____	It _____	He _____
They _____	I _____	We _____

Write the English word in the blank

invierno _____
otoño _____
primavera _____
verano _____
frío _____
calor _____
fresco _____
nublado _____
soleado _____
viento _____

Complete the following sentences using the correct form of the verb "to be" (am, is, are).
Ejemplo: It *is* cloudy tonight...

It _____ cold outside today.
The weather _____ warm in May.
It _____ windy this morning.
Kansas _____ hot in the summer.
It _____ sunny this afternoon.
The climate in Costa Rica _____ rainy in June.

Complete the following sentences using the verb "to be" and a location.
Ejemplo: It *is cloudy outside*.

The weather _____.
The climate _____.
The climate in Kansas _____.

Use complete sentences and the verb "to be" to answer the following questions.
Ejemplo: Where is the pencil? **It is on the table.**

What is the climate like in El Salvador? It is _____.
What is the weather like in the winter? _____.
What is it like outside today? _____.
What is the weather like today? _____.

Lesson 12: Weather
Vocabulary Practice

| weather climate spring | summer fall winter | cold cool warm | hot sunny rain | clouds wind snow |

Write the English word next to the Spanish word with the same meaning.

_____ nubes _____ lluvia _____ frío
_____ invierno _____ clima _____ viento
_____ soleado _____ fresco _____ otoño
_____ clima _____ nieve _____ calor
_____ cálido _____ verano _____ primavera

Copy each English vocabulary word three times.

author's bio/biografía del autor

Jarrett Meek is the founder and Executive Director of Mission Adelante, Inc, an urban ministry for immigrants and refugees in Kansas City, KS. A graduate of Midwestern Baptist Seminary, Jarrett served for several years on the staff of Heartland Community Church in Overland Park, Kansas before moving to Latin America with his wife and two daughters to work as missionaries. When they returned, they found a mission field right here at home. Jarrett has a unique gift for language learning and a special passion for serving, sharing life, and sharing Jesus with people from all places. The Meek family lives in Kansas City, Kansas and has grown to include four children.

Jarrett Meek es el fundador y Director Ejecutivo de Mission Adelante, Inc. un ministerio para inmigrantes y refugiados en Kansas City, KS. Graduado de Midwestern Baptist Seminary, Jarrett sirvió durante varios años en el equipo de trabajo de Heartland Community Church en Overland Park, Kansas, antes de mudarse a Latinoamérica con su esposa y dos hijas para trabajar como misioneros. Cuando regresaron, encontraron un campo misionero aquí en su propia ciudad. Jarrett tiene una habilidad fuerte de aprender idiomas y una pasión especial para servir, convivir, y compartir Jesús con gente de todos lugares. La familia Meek vive en Kansas City, Kansas y ha crecido a incluir a cuatro hijos.

Made in the USA
Columbia, SC
17 November 2023

26683983R00050